MW01121040

Jack,

I'm forever grateful
for your mentoring &
friendship, & your
own books, which
have taught me so
much...

Dan
1/20/2012

A Plum Tree in Leatherstocking Country

Daniel Bowman, Jr.

VIRTUAL ARTISTS COLLECTIVE
http://vacpoetry.org
ISBN: 978-0-9830091-6-0

Cover photo by Stephen A. Wolfe, "Jasper-Pulaski Sunrise," used by
permission of the photographer: http://www.flickr.com/photos/swolfe/

Interior art and book design by Steven Schroeder: stevenschroeder.org

Poems in this collection have appeared in the following publications:

*The Adirondack Review, American Poetry Journal, Art House America,
The Bitter Oleander, Cha: An Asian Literary Journal* (Hong Kong),
Flourish, Istanbul Literary Review (Turkey), *Main Street Rag, The
Midwest Quarterly, The Northern Agrarian, The Other Journal, Pyrta*
(India), *Rio Grande Review, Seneca Review,* and *Words on Walls
Literary Fresco*

All haiku are from *Cherry Blossoms: Japanese Haiku Series III* (The
Peter Pauper Press: Mount Vernon, 1960).

I would like to thank the following people, without whom this book
would not have been possible: Jud Decker, Harold Hurley, Michael
Landrum, Nick Lykling, Thom Ward, John Drury, Don Bogen, CD
Wright, John Leax, Gregory Wolfe, Jeanine Hathaway, Jeanne Murray
Walker, and the rest of the Seattle Pacific University MFA program
faculty, as well as visiting faculty to the Whidbey Island residency and the
Glen Workshop in Santa Fe. Thank you to the English Department at
Houghton College and the English Department at Taylor University.
Thank you to Jason and Katie Woodson for creating my website. Thank
you to my family: Dan Bowman Sr. and Jeanne Bowman; Bill, Matt, and
Sarah; Paul and Gail Whittaker; Em and Gabe; and Timmy and Josh.
Thank you always to my brilliant wife Beth and our children Una and
Casey: you inspire me to live and write better every day. And thank you to
many friends who have increased us at every stage of our journey.

For Beth and Una and Casey

Contents

I. Into Autumn Dusk

II. Winter-Wasted Fields

III. Old Eloquence

IV. In My Native Place

I

Into Autumn Dusk

By abandoned roads
this lonely poet marches
into autumn dusk.

—Basho

Poem for the Undead

Mohawk comes
like blackbirds at dawn,
weaves itself
into itself
like a twisted weeping willow,
face delicate,
curled as ivy,
Mohawk comes like
some small creature hit
and left for dead,
gray eyes fixed,
Mohawk bites the hills
like a river,
smokes like your kin
at the diner in the gorge,
hunched over ham and potatoes,
hidden like shadows
on back roads,
Mohawk comes.

Hammond's Farm, Mohawk

By the salt pile the scarecrow dances.
As the right hand rises,
you might recall the breaking
of the cellar window.

Hammond taps the maple
by the ruins of his grandfather's barn.
When the right hand rises,
he forgets to check the mail.

What scares me
is not ruin
but the absence of music and
the ways I can ignore it.

But the right hand rises
and the songs of our mothers
will once again pierce
the hard light shining in the kitchen.

Late September, Rochester

This place is a longing,
downtown its lonely form,
the great lake my only body.

And I am haunted by the fall,
by another generation
of murderers and thieves,

by the deaths of our fathers.
Mohawk! Tell me again,
is your moon still crisp on the river?

I left you, and here I am, away.
  I will burn through you.
      My jacket is already on fire.

Ghosts of Men

Sitting like a devil in the bell tower
at St. Christopher's,
a man watches his brother
get off the 17 in Over-the-Rhine,
looking serious but lost,
his brother who'd never been to Cincinnati,
disliked cities as a rule,
and had taken his breakfast alone.

The man knows that in a few moments
his brother will look a little helpless.
Unable to bear the thought,
he descends the stone stairs,
runs down the street,
finally reaching his brother,
asking him breathlessly, "Can I help you?"

"What? No, no," his brother says quickly.
"I'm waiting for my brother.
It's his wedding day."
His brother turns away, lights a cigarette,
belly full of fried eggs.

The man walks the twelve blocks to the river.
He follows its bend with his eyes; he doesn't look across.

To a Famous Poet with a Bad Poem in a Famous Magazine

That field behind the barn
across the road,
how it once perfected your desires
in summer sun...

To sit in that grass right now,
would you offer up a poem?
Let the eyes of orioles fund you—
let the wind publish you on leaves?

Okay, draw one more sip
of your mint julep,
and better make it a good one
because what if tonight

someone sneaks into your office,
swallows your celebrated ink pens,
and the stuffs the jar
with the barbed quills of a dead porcupine?

Diner, Midtown Manhattan

The thought that she can't stay beautiful much longer
on cigarettes and coffee
nags at her a little more
now that it's fall.
But not today.
Early Sunday morning, the city forgives her
in its light and silence.
This is how it worships—
a holy refraining,
nothing banging together.
Even the small man at the counter barely chews.

After making a promise
I knew I wouldn't keep

I walk by the canal,
by old men playing checkers.

The paint on their table peels;
dead leaves gather at their feet.

I brought my harmonica
to play under the bridge

but when I get there
I feel embarrassed,

hold it inside my pocket,
try instead to remember a poem

by Emanuel di Pasquale, try
to make a connection

between a mossy tree stump
and a little girl who's crying.

The mother's black hair
blows across her face.

I think she might smile,
though in the end she doesn't.

Then under the bridge I hear something
(an echo of the blues?)

and the old men playing checkers
sit still for a very long time

and the smooth bank's mud
resembles my father's forehead

on Saturday afternoons in summer
when he smoked cigars and chopped Box Elder.

Walking Through the Dream of a Stranger

Now I dream that I'm the stranger
    in someone else's dream,
that I'm walking
    through the dream of a stranger
and the stranger's dream turns out like
    dreams I had when I was young
where I meet a girl on a hillside
    and she loves me
and takes my hand and smiles
    and I smile too
because I love her and because
    the stranger's dream smells like
wet birch bark and crabapples
    trampled in early September.

Late October, Cincinnati

When the rain started,
I thought about home.

Walking to work in the dark
I saw a cardinal fly easily
from the sidewalk to a high branch.

Then the rain started
and I thought about home.

Then I became very hungry
and wanted to eat
at least three things—
perhaps the bird, the tree, and my job.

Somewhere in Chicago, Sometime in the Fall

He stumbles drunk
around a Polish neighborhood
on the north side.
His girlfriend
has been cheating on him
for two years.
Today she told him
then packed up and left.
He kicks a garbage can
in an empty street
but it's plastic and the sound
doesn't satisfy.
He vomits hot dogs
into a storm drain;
he rips a poster
off a telephone pole and wipes his face,
caring nothing for advertisement.

What Comes Next

Worthless Monday morning,
I've wasted you all the same,
ignored October yellow,
leaning pines
and their tones too.
Brushed off
the very field of my redemption
just because it's vulgar.
Thought more of rusty mailboxes
than cloud textures,
how they shade
the stupid strips of earth
we made then left to die.

I'm done with it.
Tonight I'll consider
evening drizzle
and lamplight.
I'll be your student, check myself
till I fall in step
with the black pace of your stillness,
because you know what comes next.

II

Winter-Wasted Fields

Feeble, feeble sun...
it can scarcely stretch across
winter-wasted fields.

—Bakusui

The Wait

November sits in the cupboard
with the tinfoil and sandwich bags.
It's after dusk.
I'm riding in the back seat,
down the back roads.

Some houses are dark.
Some have one light on
and I can't help wondering
who is doing what in that light.

The snow makes me sleepy.
There's a dream:
a woman with plum-black hair—
a bit of a local celebrity—
standing at the sink.
Without looking in the mirror,
she cups her hands,
fills them with warm water.
I am small.
I swan dive
from the tip of her nose
into her pool and open my eyes,
floating on the wait.

November straddles plum-black fields.
November waits for me,
its shadows like dreams in the dry stubble.

Behind Our Fathers' Piece Counts

We wandered the valley's
armed solitude
behind our fathers' piece counts—
100 pitchforks,
200 snow shovels,
300 shotguns—

behind skull and ice
and rusty swing sets,
the Tuesday pot roast,
an ambush of sacrifice.

The nights spilled over bluffs
and we took the laugher's oath
as the sky turned winter,
the rain to a snow
that muffled new footsteps.

Monkey Bars

These words rise, follow me
like smoke.

No sheep graze
in the field by the playground
where monkey bars sit snow-covered.

At Sangertown Square
shoppers busy themselves
in giving,
save surprises for last.
At least that's my guess;
I haven't left the house.

Hunters drive by.
At least I think they're hunters.
What are they hunting?
Disguised by the white curtain
wrapped around my shoulders,
I stand at the window,
eyeball this procession
of camouflaged death-men.

I'm here.
You can tell by
the breadcrumbs on the cutting board.

Winter Fog

December, in the freeze,
    I walk across the fields above the valley.

Herkimer:
    a white cross marks my grandfather's grave.

Below the crumbling smokestacks of Frankfort
    my father rolls pitchforks.

My mother sees patients
    in trailers near Cedarville.

Across the river, a cluster of lights
    recalls the shoulders of my brother.

The Thruway is closed
    from Utica to Syracuse.

The fog, great ghost of an old Mohawk winter,
    burns before I reach it.

Father Adams' Ghost Plays Jazz Bassoon

The stranger is sitting in the corner and I'm at a table in front. Father Adams notices neither of us; when he looks up at all, it's at the door. He's expecting someone, and he's playing jazz bassoon with a vigor only realized by the ghost of the priest of one's childhood. In the mural behind him, the great purple fish swims in circles without compromising its trademark sense of misery.

Finally, the jingling of the bell. A girl walks in, her head shaved, a pair of wings tattooed to the back of her neck. She's tall—taller even than the formidable ghost of Father Adams, which goes about six-three, and now leans toward the floor, hoisting the impressive mass of the bassoon in a burst of improvisation. The bass crashes against me like a wave, stumbles and drifts through my ribs till I'm dizzy. But the girl, she looks at Father Adams, then the stranger, then me, then the fish; I observe her teeth and tongue as they say nothing to no one.

Now she offers up an unusually puffy cloud of smoke. It swells, rises to the rafters, I watch it, I look down, she's gone, everyone's gone, the door to the alley is propped open and the wind whisks in and I am alone except for the stranger sitting in the corner, legs crossed, tasting winter air.

December in Middle America

Just before Christmas
     in blue and red
there's a moment
     when my soul knows perfectly
its own emptiness.
     That the last shall be the first
and the first, last is no matter:
     I smell hot rolls and coffee,
and do not long for the shore.

New York Winter

Tonight the ancient lovemaker
plays the songs I can't hear.
I know this
because I imagine the soft tones
of his guitar.

In the morning
I won't see his footprints in the snow,
or him stooping
to grab the newspaper
in which every story whispers his birth.

The whole business is a shame, really,
because his only passion is to reach me.

But who cares?
He's always been a liar and a drunk.

The Sticking

Snow falls into the long gray.

Walking alone
through the town of my birth
makes everything
stick to my feet.
Soon I've got Blessed Sacrament
on my right heel,
basket of blue fish flopping
eternal, a young confessor
falling, clinging
to the scarlet curtain.
On my left,
between my toes:
Montana House,
pool balls rolling hard
for the bumper,
Utica Club sign spitting neon
at a woman who'll be kneeling
across the street tomorrow.

If you're coming this way,
slow down:
I'm sure to block traffic
in both directions
at least for a few minutes
while I get the sticking under control.

When the mailman dies

no one will be left, not even you,
since all these years
I wrote love letters
I knew you'd never read
and I was right,
except I thought you'd keep them
in a shoebox
under the swooning couch
and on this count I was mistaken
because the mailman stole them—
that short fellow
with the hairy ears.

I'd forgotten
until the day
he sauntered up the walk
and I understood what happened,
indeed, how it must've been.

I was listening to Larry Clinton,
who'd often been accused of
a flimsy saxophone section.
The great Bea Wain
sang Stormy Weather
The mailman knocked.
Truth time.
Come in, I said,
Would you like coffee?

He accepted,
coyly, I thought.
Buffalo, he muttered,
that's where Harold Arlen was born.
Only a guy from Buffalo could pen
Stormy Weather.
I responded,
Okay, you rotten bastard,
where are they?

This is the blackest coffee I've ever had,
he observed.
Where'd you get it?

On the bottom of the Genesee River,
I said, there's a hole that goes down
to the center of the earth
and that's where I get my coffee.

Then that's where they are, he said.
They've always been there.
It's not my fault
and you know it.

With apologies to Lena Horne,
I said, this is the better version
of the tune.
Quite right, said the mailman.

Good afternoon, sir, I replied,
and thank you for the coffee.

We don't serve coffee at the post office,
someone said.
Hi, I said, three first-class stamps please.
I've got some letters that need to go out
right away.
Very good, someone said.

Till Spring Comes

Stay by the window.
    Forsake brass,
        perhaps even woodwinds:
our secret country
    will die on a cello.
        Our hands will break
at the insistence of violins.
    Our eyes must close
        like church doors
so the fractious sun
    can drink us. Stay by the window
        till spring comes.

Hymn for a Mohawk January

Ashes bring hard faith:
in my vision, only the late nigrescence,
the symphony at Stanwix,
and always the open field.

I cross the street,
ignoring light from the corner.
And here, still, my shocked valley
of pumps and furnaces raging.

III
Old Eloquence

Silent cherry-bloom...
again with your old eloquence
address my inner ear.

—Onitsura

The Girl and the Hill

This is the year
the bodiless balladmonger
will make her ascent
up the hill called Saraboche
on a trail
where there exists
no history of gymnastics,
no syrupy resistance
half-whispered
in a carpeted basement.

This is the year
she will move as she is,
lit by broken autumns
and painted by the drifts—
no Daughters of the American Revolution,
no converts, no lessons,
no wounded animals,
not even distant obsessions
crowned from her February.

Early March: Bay Ridge, Brooklyn

Rain-patter beyond
the striped awning,
a bowl of hot noodles
and jasmine tea—
is that a trumpet
drifting from the brick?
A girl singer on the chorus?

We devour our noodles and
suck orange slices,
feeling extravagant.
We're broke
but our toes won't know until morning
when we say yes to the earth.

April Poem

Every year about this time
I bury my mother's bones.
And in May
they spring up as lilacs
and in June they float softly

on the Irondequoit Creek
and in July they march down
Columbia Street
and end with smoke.
In August they become

Poison Ivy creeping
along the trail where I walk
with my daughter.
Soon they'll be hidden
under dead leaves and snow.

The thaw will have its say
again next year
and I'll reach for the shovel,
happy for moonlight
and a grasshopper's song.

The Hunger

plays jazz
in the dark, bass
like a bear
in a cave
reeling
through water.

My memories
of love
fool me again
like the man
smoking
and talking
on the phone

who seems
both always
and never there,
by the poster
that reads

FRIDAY NIGHT:
THE HUNGER

The Poet Goes Before the Board of Directors

This is all a misunderstanding.
You see, at present there is a great deal
of corruption in that part of the world.
Yes, I'm aware I was sent there
to conduct research for poems.

Yes, I perceive the "appreciable distance,"
as you call it, between the stated goals
of my accepted proposal
and the results my visit yielded.

The hotel manager
claimed I made offensive remarks
to his daughter. Who is
much younger than she appears, I would add.
At that point I did in fact seek out
the Institute, and was turned away—
disparagingly, I would add.

Sure, my face was bloody—
I'd had a tooth knocked out, you know.
I assure you, any alcohol consumed
was strictly in the service of pain management.
Regardless, it seems I may have failed
to relay my story to the Institute
in a manner deemed convincing,
and...no, I would *not*
characterize my behavior as belligerent.

Perhaps uncouth.
I was greatly distressed.
And yet I was ready to put all of that behind me,
to get cleaned up and do some good work.
That's correct—the work for which
you so generously awarded the grant.
I needed a bath and a shave and a decent meal.
Having no place to go,
I wandered into a village outside the city,
became thoroughly lost,
hungry, at which point,
in a fit of despair, I stole the hen.
You see I tripped on a bicycle tire
as I ran away.
Yes, the hen broke free
and that's when the woman fired the shot.

It seems the circus was in town.
Enormous trucks blocked the streets
as men set up tents.
It was all very confusing.
One couldn't know whom one could trust.
And the awful heat...
an acrobat
running morning errands
stepped across my body.
She dropped her bananas
then reached down and
picked them up
and walked away.

The people stood in line
eating peanuts
and holding their children's hands,
all ignoring me
except one little boy
with very large, serious eyes.
He prayed over me,
prayed for "a simple ministry."
Yes, I'm certain that is what he said.
No, I do not understand what it means.
No, I suppose I cannot give you a reason
why I should be trusted.
No, I do not understand what it means.

Delaware Sky

Silent as the salt that saw me born

at sea's edge

when breathing was worship,

heavy in the tide's foam,

glistening with new sun:

Delaware sky,

orange and blue by turns.

Song to Cincinnati

In the piney plunge of Clifton
 the doctors' dogs are restless.

From the hill at Mount Storm
 I hear them howl.

Indiana clouds roll low
 across the train yard.

Like dreams the stone walls
 recess in deep divides.

This time, no one's talking
 about wolves

or the fields above the valley,
 peppered with handsprings.

In your hidden playground,
 Cincinnati, we burn our circles.

In your lime and silver
 we trust the river's ballad.

Your Room

It's man's curse to be lame in life,
woman's to unfold. I do.

—Adélia Prado

In your room
you will sleep without harassment
of nightmare.
Your room will have eight walls,
at least—the final plans
may well call for more—
no, seven walls (an odd number
is clearly preferable in this case)—
no, wait: no walls!

And of course no ceiling.
But a floor that is wonderfully cool
though never cold,
and certainly each wall
will support glorious windows
and window seats for reading
and the most interesting
crannies so that you
will not tire of the room.
One must feel that one could die here,
which as you know
may become necessary.
Indeed that's why I will

44

personally ensure that the windows
on each wall
will look upon
many different types of trees!

You seem unhappy.
I don't get it.
Isn't this what you wanted?

I hate to say it,
but, you know,
most people would give anything
for a room like this.
Only this one is *yours*, your very own.

A butterfly conservatory
at the west end?
Now you're talking!
Of course. I should've thought of it.
Good, good—your input is critical, as you know.
After all, this is for you; it's your room.

Kings of the Valley

Buy candy for the kids
whose eyes gleam
from the Shultz and Dooley.
The streets of Mohawk
are not hash marks on a football field.
They're Iroquois paths,
towpaths on the river,
and the lonely farming accidents
of the dead.

You kings who moved in the dark,
are you there anymore
in sumac and maple
by your open fires?
Do you still buy candy for the kids
who know only where the sky ends
and pierce you with the thorns of love?

Or have you burned already
like the morning fog
in the fields above the valley,
above the Iroquois paths
and the lonely farming accidents
of the dead?

Night Walking, Seattle

Church bells
drunk with grace
cut the spring moon.

The walker shoves damp hands
to pocket ends, passes
forbidden places
and the useless distances between.

Back home
in the horn of the valley,
creek waters foam on black rocks.

On a Ranch in Northern Arkansas

Today I clear limbs
left from last night's storm.
The morning sun calms,
as if it never happened.
The buffalo have relaxed.
The pigs look happy.
A small goat has freed himself
and will need to be retrieved.

The ride from the ranch
to the farm
is hot and dusty.
When we cross the creek,
the dog knows what to do.

It's just us out here
for miles.
Sap has hardened
on my hands, neck, jaw,
and in the bend of my arm.

My Father

His shadow, bronze,
floats near the bank
of the Mohawk River.

IV
In My Native Place

In my native place
there's this plant: as plain as grass
but blooms like Heaven.

—Issa

Passing

for Hannah Wronkoski Dillon

Something is sinking
behind the heather and laurel,
in the moment between
quarrel and dream.
No one notices.
We can't; it's hidden.
Only the silent voice suggests
that to forget
what we never saw,
to un-know what we never knew,
is the way of things.
Yet
behind the heather and laurel
something is sinking
and emptiness rises in its place,
tiny as a needle's eye
through which we, all of us,
will pass like thread.

Directions

Head right through the toothed wheel,
through going home,
through can't go home again,

out toward the scarred fir
and the leaning poplar.
At the bridge you'll hear
your uncle laugh as he deflects
an onslaught of marshmallows.

The only way from there
is directly into the creek.
Then go up the hill
and trace the crow-black
abandoned strip mall parking lot's
Pollack-stripes of tar
into the humid expanse
until nothing has a name.

It may seem like you're going
in a circle.
That's perfectly natural;
you're almost there.
Just bang a hard left
through your father's Jersey City
and turn wide
around your mother's ear,
through the cigarettes and pigeons.

At this point,
you'll be under the compass.
Which is not being lost
and also is not somewhere but not nowhere.

Oswegatchie River Blues

Each boy eats his bread,
rides by evergreens.
      Each boy sees his sleep
from the road
and sends an echo,

believes that stars
      are pink and warm.

Thirteen chances in the Oswegatchie:
      hide your face
if you see your sleep from the water.

Poem about Baseball

for Aubrey Pennington

The Yankees lost but it's only July and we're thirsty,
we flee the Bronx, switch trains at midtown, take the
Q all the way to Sheepshead Bay, wander into the
bar closest to the stop which seems to be some kind
of cosmic tennis club for models who speak only
Russian. Being short and Irish and you being black
we exchange a look, scan the taps for the least
conspicuous brew but no one in the place is drinking
beer, we settle on Coronas, the third goes down
smoothly and man the music is loud and now
someone's dancing and of course we love these crazy
Russians and they prize us as mascots, hearty
vagabonds, turns out they're charitable, vodka for all,
we've become objects of delight on a hot Saturday
night and how I wish I knew an old Russian drinking
song to end things right. We're happy all the way
back to 23rd Street. The Yankees lost but it's only July.

On the Shore Just After Sunset

I'm having a cheeseburger and a beer
at Lucky Jim's
on the shore just after sunset
when I see myself
through the window faintly, barefoot
and unshaven among the seagulls
at water's edge, kneeling over
my body
which has washed up on the rocks.

The kneeling me looks like
a man who has kept to himself
for too long upon learning
he had been fooled by a grand idea.
He repents only in the face of death.
The dead me is white as an angel,
young and crowned with seaweed.

I want to get up but I remember
I sold my feet at a trading post
in Lexington, Kentucky.
So I come barreling out
of the backroom looking annoyed

and carry myself
down to the beach where I
sit myself down next to the dead me
quietly so as not to disturb
the kneeling me, while

the me that carried me out here
rumbles back
toward the light of Lucky Jim's,
stained apron flapping in the breeze.

The New Literacy

for Jud Decker

I'm chasing birds and cats and leaves,
choosing
Old Testament heroes,
trailing apostles through Judea,
studying the moves of the Lord Himself;
I'm chasing myself
around the living room,

seeing sleepy projections—
15th-century Flemish art:
the Merode Altarpiece;
I'm running down baseballs
in the backyard,
searching for a homer
through tinseled trees,
shivering,

spiking at the calves
of long-legged cross-country runners;
I'm playing lost solos
to my best friend's twelve-string—
Brookwood Park;
it's a tag game
and still going—
Herkimer, South Washington Street Bridge,

Ilion, the back roads of Mohawk,
the cemetery,

the candle shop in Utica;
I'm hunting down day and night themselves
and climbing toward the big bands:
the elusive bari sax,
Latin percussion,
ghosts of nightclub conductors;
I'm riding shotgun

in my brother's LTD,
sinking Cobain

back to the belly,
knowing I'm being chased too,
being run out of my own town
like an outlaw
until finally,

at last,
the body becomes the name,
the words become the body,
the body, the body,
the thousand versions of warmth.

Cymbals

We washed windows for doctors.
Pigeons scattered.
Fridays were busy—
six birds on a cupola.

We scrubbed rusty cast iron
in office courtyards.
Wednesdays were cloudy
and we were not knights
and we were not
scattering pigeons.
Wednesdays were busy,
a leaking roof,
the footer for a salesman's steps,
16's in the corner of my mouth.

We clawed cedar shakes
on a steeple downtown.
A parade sounded around the corner.
People lined the street;
their team must've won that year,
won it all while we'd fallen behind,
seeing only the accidents of our tools.

Swimming

When the sun goes blue
I drown again.
I drown all day because
the lake is my body
and the city's a mirror.
When I sneeze,
the trout flip.
When I blink,
the seaweed sways.

Once
when I wasn't being careful
I tripped over the curb
and heard a man
fall out of his boat.
Instead of returning to the vessel,
he began swimming
rather calmly
toward the sun.
That's how I knew
it was my father, and now I know
where he's been all these years.

A Plum Tree in Leatherstocking Country

for my grandmother

Her throat is Christmas carols;
her feet are the mice in the breezeway.
Her thumbs are kindling— her mouth,
the last question in the Mohawk Valley.

In the East Herkimer of her childhood,
clapboards are peeling, bread is stale,
teeth sharp and meatless,
and thoughts, not words, swell to fat.

When did the plum tree die? I ask.
It fought hard, she tells me.
Odd anyway, she says,
a plum tree in Leatherstocking Country.

Daniel Bowman Jr.'s work has appeared in journals in the US and around the world, including *The Adirondack Review, American Poetry Journal, The Bitter Oleander, Cha: An Asian Literary Journal* (Hong Kong), *Istanbul Literary Review* (Turkey), *Main Street Rag, The Midwest Quarterly, The Other Journal, Pyrta* (India), *Rio Grande Review, Rock & Sling, Seneca Review*, and others. He holds an MA in Comparative Literature from the University of Cincinnati and an MFA in Creative Writing from Seattle Pacific University. He was raised in the Mohawk River Valley of upstate New York. He lives with his wife Beth and their two children in central Indiana, where he teaches at Taylor University.

CPSIA information can be obtained at www.ICGtesting.com
Printed in the USA
LVOW071241150112

263895LV00004B/5/P

What they're saying about *A Plum Tree in Leatherstocking Country*:

"Daniel Bowman Jr.'s poetry is as American as Walt Whitman and Emily Dickinson and Chief Seattle blended in the prairies and lakes and mountains and the passion of the American spirit, from New York across the wide land. It is always human and it sings splendidly, rich in animistic mystery. I delight in these poems. Bowman has a great big heart and finds himself home in the lyrical brotherhood."

- **Emanuel di Pasquale**, translator and author of *Writing Anew: New and Selected Poems*

"In his first collection of poems, Dan Bowman describes quotidian moments of ordinary life and before you know it, mystery enters and twists everything. The book is haunted by ancestors and cultural memories and premonitions and ghosts. It captures brilliantly the strangeness of being human. Let these poems stand as a warning and a promise. There's no predicting what will happen: a plum tree is, yes, blossoming in Leatherstocking Country."

- **Jeanne Murray Walker**, author of *New Tracks, Night Falling*

To see our full poetry catalogue, visit http://vacpoetry.org/.